Off
Our Rockers
By Hall Duncan, Ph.D.

A Humor for Health Publication
International Center for Humor and Health

To Lois
for her encouraging laughter, boundless sense of humor,
creative perspective and enthusiastic support.

OFF OUR ROCKERS

© 1998 Hall F. Duncan, Ph.D.

Typesetting by Word Works
Book Design by Humor in Communication

Library of Congress Catalog Card Number: 98-70391
ISBN: 0-9661367-1-3

Published by
International Center for Humor and Health
2930 Hidden Valley Road
Edmond, Oklahoma 73013

Foreword

Research from all over the globe is indicating that Laughter is indeed good medicine. It reduces stress, promotes physical healing, boosts immunity, relieves pain, encourages mental health, decreases anxiety, enhances communication, and inspires creativity.

Hall Duncan is a wonderful ambassador for the healing power of humor. He had dedicated his life to bringing joy to the lives of others.

He has worked tirelessly on every continent teaching laughter as a life skill. He teaches laughter as a coping mechanism to help stem the suicide problem in Japan. He teaches laughter as a social lubricant to help relieve the racial tension in the United States and South Africa. He teaches all over the world how to use laughter in the classroom to become better teachers.

Hall is now sharing with us, as we get older, the regenerative power of laughter. His message: "Get off your rocker, laugh at yourself and live life to the fullest."

I am grateful for Hall Duncan. I am grateful he has blessed us with more laughter through "Off Our Rockers".

You'll be tickled, too!

Jim Fite, MBA
Executive Director
International Center
for Humor and Health

Between the Laughs and Groans . . .

This book has been bouncing around in my mind for years. I suppose it's because I was living most of it bumbling through my own real life absurdities and observing those of others.

At any rate, here it is. Hopefully you will be laughing more than groaning. Both depend on your mood and frame of mind as you turn these pages.

My goal is to help you who are over fifty-five to rediscover joy and fun in your lives. Humor is a way we can cope with hope and survive feeling that this magnificent gift of life is worth the trip. And it is. I never miss a day thanking God for breath and our ability to smile and laugh.

Recently, while traveling on Turner Turnpike in Oklahoma, I observed a parade of all sorts of people to and from the counter at a McDonalds. I then went to the restroom and looked into the mirror and asked, "God, do I belong to this really funny world?" And, in a flash He said: "You certainly do. Now get back out there. You're one of them!"

That's what I'm doing in this book. Have fun!

Hall Duncan

"Our laughter makes our world a happier place!"

4

Been There . . . Done That . . . I Think I Remember!

Ah, To Be A Grandparent!
Are You Maintaining Your Sanity?

A headline caught my attention in our local paper: "Many Unprepared for Parenthood, Expert Says!" Does that ring a bell as you recall having your first child? It did me, as well as the other three that followed. I get tired thinking about it, particularly feeding the twins at 3 a.m.

The article prompted me to think about grandparents. How prepared are we for "grandparenthood?" Kind of scary, isn't it?

I congratulate you grandparents who have had the job of raising your grandkids full-time. You deserve a medal. You can teach the rest of us a lot.

Do grandparents have a formula for raising a happy, secure grandkid? I decided to do some very unscientific research by interviewing grandparents and myself. The results are interesting and take off in several directions.

First, children will tell their grandparents what's really going on in their parents' homes. They are a great source for the real news, sort of a Washington Post at domestic level. That's one big benefit of baby-sitting.

Also, what you do with your grandchild is more important to the child than what you say. You really raise eyebrows when word gets back that you taught your three-year-old granddaughter how to play poker.

Next, as a grandparent, you must have an exceptionally strong nose as you change a kid whose diaper has been unattended for hours because you took him to a three-hour movie. And when it comes to teaching the little ones how to blow their noses properly, remember you've got to "honk your horn" many times, almost to the point of nose bleed.

A grandfather in a small town told me that the trouble with most grandkids today, including his, is that they are being raised not reared. He defined "reared" as spanking a kid's bottom when it did something really bad. He said "raised" implied "time out" when the child was horribly naughty, adding that the latter punishment is for the politically correct family. I was reared as a child. How about you?

Being a grandparent these days can be a lot of fun, and yet very trying. We need to take care of ourselves to avoid burnout..

"Honey, Mother's here to babysit!"

One grandmother gave me her following four point survival guide:

1. When your grandchild is in the terrible twos and threes age bracket, leave the country or reside in some inaccessible spot in the mountains of Montana. Do not have a forwarding address or phone. Let your children know that you'll be available to baby-sit again when the grandchildren are four or older, and that you still love them.

2. Baby-sit infrequently. Once a month is fine. You are better rested. It also makes it more difficult for your grandchild to discover your weak spots in order to completely control you.

3. Baby-sit for only a short duration. A few hours or a weekend at the most. The reason is so you can return the grandkids back to their parents for any major correction.

4. When you take your grandkids out to eat, be prepared to give your waitress a big, generous tip to cover the clean-up of spilled drinks and catsup all over the place. You'll leave with a clear conscience.

Grandparents need to be extremely careful in telling their children how to raise the grandkids. For example, my stepmother enjoyed baby-sitting for very short periods of time, particularly when the kids were tiny and cuddly. She advised my brother, Jim, and his wife, Barbara, that they were not raising their children correctly.

After thinking it over, they called her and said: "You're absolutely right! We want you to come over and take care of the kids for two weeks straight while we go on vacation alone." They never heard another word from her on child care. Somehow they were seen to be raising their kids the right way!

Grandparents represent family tradition. I remember my grandmother, Myrtiller Hall, gathering us grandkids around her chair on the living room rug and telling us stories. She kept us spellbound with her tales of growing up on the prairie and raising her large family on a southern Kansas farm.

Our eyes widened as she related how the Indians came to her home to eat, and they always ate their dessert first. I liked that idea so much that I began to do likewise. My mother became extremely upset. "Hall, stop that. Eat your vegetables and meat first. Who taught you to do that?" With sheepish delight, I said, "Your Mother." I learned fast at an early age what grandparents are for.

As my kids grew up, I was happy about my children's respect for family tradition, until the day my son, Frank, asked to borrow an old suit belonging to his grandfather. He wanted it for a school party. He was going as John Dillinger, a notorious American bank robber of the 1930's.

The other night during the whining of a grandchild whose sobs were as phony as a three dollar bill, I determined that she wasn't sick or hurt, so I started sobbing in my falsetto voice letting her know I too had feelings about my imagined injury and could see right through her scheme to get my dander up. Praise God! She stopped! The game of intimidation was over, and we enjoyed our meal together.

My grandchildren are an energizing retirement benefit when I laugh with them. As I reach the end of a session of baby-sitting, I realize that I need to be more creative by inventing exciting new activities to strengthen a positive bonding.

Don't we all want to see the same thing? Grandchildren behaving like "grand" children. But doesn't it haunt us, knowing that we, like they, have gone through this long trying process of struggling from one stage of life to another? By laughing more, through it all, we can look forward to our next encounter of "fun" with our grandkids and start over again.

"No, sweetie, that's not your ball. That's Grandfather!"

9

"These safety helmets sure do come in handy!"

"Grandmother won't give me my turn!"

"Notice how my grandson looks like a gentleman since his grandfather's been dressing like a bum!"

"Okay, super-girl wins again. Grandmother monster is dead!"

"See, I told you my grandson plays 'tailback' for his school!"

"We'll sell more tickets if you let your granddaughter do her act alone!"

There's Nothing Like A Hobby
To Keep Us Out of Trouble!

A few years ago I was conducting a program entitled "Other Mount Everests" for retirees. My purpose was to inspire these folks to enrich their lives by improving relationships with their spouses and friends. I encouraged them to lighten up, laugh and explore.

I suggested one excellent way was to have a hobby they really enjoyed. A poll was taken to see how many had hobbies. And sure enough most all were doing something . . . collecting antiques, stamps, refinishing furniture, and so on. One silver haired lady in the front row said "Here's my hobby!" pointing to her husband who was virtually half way to a sound sleep. We all laughed.

Her idea has some real merit to it. Why not begin to collect life-filling experiences by living them? Adopting a hobby of making friends and sharing the fun. The happiest people I know are doing just that. Laughter is contagious.

Collecting things, if taken too far, can be a problem. Years ago, I visited an elderly couple in South Africa. Their hobby was collecting magazines and newspapers. So much so that they were reduced to having their meals in a tiny corner of one room. I prayed that neither would ever sneeze. An avalanche would bury them alive!

I recall the home where a father prided his child's miniature railroad. Quite a set-up with its maze of lights, tracks, stations and towns. However, when it came time to demonstrate the railroad to me the father said to his son, "You run along and play outside while I show Mr. Duncan the railroad." Whose railroad is it anyway?

A friend of mine, a printer nearing retirement kept a model railroad in a back office. One day while visiting him there, the phone rang and I heard him say to his secretary: "If anyone calls during the next hour, I'm in conference!" . . . He winked at me. His hobby was sheer fun.

One retiree I met in Arizona had his own one man band. He had great fun banging cymbals between his knees and puffing through a harmonica wired around his neck. He refused to acknowledge that he was off key, and

"While you're waiting for Jay Leno to discover you, here's a desperate call from the Buzzard Gulch Program Committee!"

the sounds were terrible, He was a great asset to helping end a boring family reunion early when it was nap time. It was a joy to watch him as he lived his fantasy of imagining he was a star in Las Vegas.

Hobbies can be expensive, such as remaking an old model-T or Thunderbird. Searching for parts becomes quite an adventure. But it's worth it for the one hour ride in the antique car section of the Fourth of July Parade. A time when a couple can fantasize that they've been elected to be the "first family of their state," and they don't have to do a lick of work to run the government, just tinker around on their prized toy and wave in parades.

A friend wrote me from Arkansas about his hobby of restoring antique cars. He wrote "These cars keep me in the garage, out of the bars, and away from wild women!" his wife says, "Amen to that!"

Some retired folks take another job and call it a hobby because they haven't found anything else that suits them. And the wife feels her prayer is answered when "Mr. Bored-to-Death" gets out of the house several times a week to serve hamburgers at McDonalds or welcome folks to Wal-Mart. He feels he's appreciated and being paid for it.

Hobbies reveal our uniqueness. I'm all for that. Some men and women I know serve as clowns entertaining the lonely in nursing homes and children recovering in hospitals. Others achieve national news by their recipes for sweet potato pie or running a doll hospital. However, if you want to be really far-out, train some caterpillars to do a gymnastic routine. I guarantee such hobbies create laughter, and you will be in the National Enquirer. Front page!.

A hobby can be almost anything. It's all up to you and me! Our main concern is to make sure it keeps us out of trouble and leaves us enough money for groceries, aspirins for our arthritis and our grandchildren. Come to think of it, our grandchildren and their parents are the all-consuming hobby for most of us older folks. Right?

*"Eleanor, your obsession for elephants means
I'll have to sleep in the bathroom!"*

"And how's my top banana today?"

"How clever! She's exhibiting her husband!"

"Fred lost interest and now we have a new guest room!"

*"Yes, Leonard, you are a genius, but your
one-a-year vitamin tablet is not going to fly!"*

"The response is awesome since I misspelled sax-o-phone as sex-o-phone on my web page!"

"Do you realize you've made our kitchen into the 18th green, and I've got to fix supper now?"

Sometimes I Get Ill
Just Trying to Stay Healthy!

I am very grateful for the many advances in medical technology, such as heart transplants and procedures dealing with cancer and other serious diseases. But there is another plague that haunts many a senior in trying to get a doctor to look at him or her.

It's the waiting that wears us out. I believe that doctors' waiting rooms could be more cheerful with cartoons on the wall and music piped in that makes us want to tap our feet and dance. Even an interlude on the hour where nurses belt out a kind of "Happy Days Are Here Again" songs. I heard about one patient who asked to be left totally alone. She said she enjoyed feeling lousy. What a sense of humor!

One of my dear friends, whom I'll call Jane, was devastated to learn that she had breast cancer. It was life threatening. Both she and her husband were in shock. She called me and over the following months I was in contact with her before and after the operation. Depression engulfed her. We decided to use a laughter plan of sharing jokes and funny incidents in our lives to help her cope. One of her major concerns was her surgeon. He never smiled in her presence. His exams were a gloom and doom experience. Why couldn't he lighten up?

To improve this situation, we made a plan. When she had her next postoperative exam, she was to wear a clown nose into his office, march right up to him, and say "Doctor, there's been a complication." She did. Like Saul being divinely thunderstruck on the road to Damascus, the doctor laughed. The relationship improved instantly between Jane and her doctor.

Thank God humor happens in some hospitals, nursing homes and wherever older folks gather. I only wish it were more often. But it takes a "clown" in the group to instigate and light up our lives. One crusty twinkle-eyed gentleman in his hospital room delighted in greeting anyone who knocked on his door with "Friend or Enema?!"

Have you ever been trapped in an elevator where seconds seem like hours? Well, it happened to me at a local hospital.

I entered an elevator with two doctors. One from India and another from Africa. The door closed. I pressed the elevator button. Nothing

"Bernie, your stomach may have given up,
but you don't have to!"

happened. I pressed it again. Nothing. We waited. Nothing. The African doctor pushed the button. Nothing. And then in true patient fashion I turned to the doctor from India and asked: "May I have a second opinion?" He pushed the button, and we were on our way up! What roaring laughter! We became energized for the rest of the day.

My pharmacist friend keeps a special room at his business where old-timers from around the town can meet regularly to swap yarns. Their stories are repeated time and again, and get better and better. They don't take life lying down. They're lying sitting up. Humor abounds as they sip their coffee and wait for their chance to tell a "big one." Blest be the yarn that bonds. The pharmacist, by providing this place to meet, dispenses a medicine that can never be bought.

Most pharmacists have a sense of humor. As I plod to mine with my anti-cholesterol prescription each month, I find him always cheerful and full of life. Recently, my urologist put me on an antibotic. When I picked up the new prescription, my pharmacist with a flashing grin, said: "I must warn you about this medicine. If you are pregnant or planning to be, it can be dangerous!" We both then laughed. But then wasn't there an insane movie recently where a man gave birth to a baby?

I wish people in the medical profession would laugh and encourage their patients to do likewise. The nurses seem to be doing a better job at it. I'm fortunate though. My gereantologist, Larry Wright, believes that a well nourished sense of humor may be among the most potent retardants of the aging process.

One way to get in shape so you feel like laughing is to go on a strict diet. "Discipline yourself!", they say. I observed a lady and her bout with unwanted pounds. She mixed up the most foul-tasting liquid I ever drank. She guaranteed it would keep a person from getting fat. Her remedy reminded me of stagnant water and licorice. She lost weight. And her secret dawned on me. She didn't eat. That stuff would take anybody's appetite.

I wish we all would enjoy each day as a gift from God and laugh at ourselves. What fun! Let's take care of ourselves with a healthy diet, lots of good exercise and a daily dose of laughter. Why get ill trying to stay healthy?

"His wife dropped him off, Doctor. He's in good health but she can't stand him today!"

"Thank God for prunes!"

"Doctor, since my last visit there's been a complication!"

"Okay, who's the wise guy imitating farm animals?"

*"I must warn you not to take these pills
if you are planning to be pregnant."*

"It's not a heart attack. This patient was doing his medical paper work!"

On The Road Again! Surprise!

Aside from the mass of eighteen wheelers streaming over the highways, we've got thousands of retirees churning their recreational vehicles down every nook and cranny in this shrinking country of ours. They all seem to be hell-bent on adventure and getting every ounce of excitement their breath and life will allow them to have. God bless 'em. They're my kind of people.

Others travel with tents, pop-up trailers or just a car loaded for bear. Each maintains their own brand of comfort from roughing it for days with no showers and cooking over an open fire to catered meals in a posh motel room next to a luxurious pool.

The problem comes when the husband and wife have such different tolerance levels in their individual comfort zones, that a vacation can become a virtual tug of war. "That motel's toilet is horrible. Won't stay there," she says. "But the price is reasonable. We can have a good three weeks on the road staying in places like this," he retorts. "And furthermore, we can build up an immunity to all diseases." "Ha," she says, "Not funny."

Back and forth and back and forth in pushing their preferences finally to a tolerable compromise they can both live with and enjoy.

Travel does involve some risks depending on where you're off to. Sometimes this can be understanding the do's and don'ts of our friends in other countries. For example, I remember when my late wife, Evelyn, and I were traveling with Korean friends in South Korea.

Evelyn excused herself from our train compartment to go to the restroom. Two minutes later she comes back very pale exclaiming "There's no stool! Just a slit hole in the floor." "But that's the way they do it here, dear," I said. "I can't do it. It just isn't right.", she replied.

Then our host, Mr. Lee, gently ushered her back to the toilet to explain how to use it and to keep from rolling over as the train rocks down the track or comes to a screeching halt. Evelyn grudgingly seemed to be resolved to bear the brunt of the toilet ordeal. And she laughed. We all laughed. It brought us all together as friends.

Most of us take too many clothes when we travel. We forget that we may end up doing our own laundry if we're on the road for several weeks in some exotic places. And then on planes you can only take so much.

However, some of us compress an enormous amount of clothing in a suitcase. The problem comes going through customs when our baggage explodes to double its size as it's opened.

"No, we're not importing limburger cheese. It's our two weeks of dirty laundry!"

What hurts is the customs officer saying, "You're fine, you can go now!" With clothes and souvenirs all over the place! You've got to be kidding!

I've observed a few seniors who say to heck with it and leave the case semi-open with socks and underwear oozing out all over the place. Also, I've noticed how a wife doesn't walk near her husband when he does this.

Once while traveling in the French-speaking Cameroon in Africa, I stayed at a guest house on top of a hill overlooking Yaounde, the capital city. Being exhausted from the heat and dust, I decided to take a shower. So for some five minutes I soaped my body to where I was totally covered with thick suds from head to toe. Now for the luxurious rinse of hot water. But no hot water. In fact, no water at all. Desperately, I climbed on top of the toilet stool lid to inspect the water pipes. Maybe something was clogged or there was a valve I could turn and get rid of this thick coat of suds. And as I reached to inspect the water intake pipe I fell through the plastic toilet seat feet first. The seat was shattered. Still no water, and my feet were jammed in the stool.

After freeing myself and wiping off as much of the soap as I could, I waited for several hours until the water came back on, and I could be clean again. I can't think of a more miserable feeling than to be covered with a thin film of soap in a hot and humid climate. But what was most embarrassing was that my travel expense account listed one plastic toilet seat, $35.00. That took a lot of explaining.

Foreign languages always present many surprises as we oldsters learn words in another mother tongue. With horror, I recall saying in French, "I'm pregnant." to a French-Canadian nun, when I meant to say "Thank you, I'm full and enjoyed the meal!"

Have you ever stayed in the homes of friends in other countries? It's quite fun, isn't it. There can be some surprises as we try our best to be the perfect guest. Be sure and write these experiences down because your kids and grandchildren will love you for it.

I remember visiting an Icelandic family in Reykjavik. Shortly after arriving in their home, we introduced ourselves, and I became particularly interested in learning the children's names.

All was going well. Then I asked "What is your baby's name?" The mother replied "Notchèt!" I said, "What a beautiful name. It sounds rather like an Eastern European name, it's so poetic!" And then loud laughter followed. Enunciating her words in English more carefully, the mother said, "Not yet. We haven't named the baby yet!" Boy, did I walk into that one. But that's all part of the surprises in being on the international highway.

Planning another travel adventure? Be ready to meet the unexpected with your sense of humor, and you'll remember them with joy.

"Surprise, Mom and Dad! The kids don't have any school this week, and I got some time off!"

"You guys certainly got carried away!"

"For some strange reason I feel at home here!"

"Well, Edwin, you sure know how to beat that traffic!"

"Everytime we come here I feel your mother doesn't like me!"

Lord, Forgive Me For
Laughing in Church

As I sat down this morning to write, I thought about what happened yesterday at a church service I was attending in a small Kansas town.

It came time for the congregation to share their joys and concerns. One long-time member stood up and said, "I have a joy and a concern. My joy is that last week my wife and I drove down to Oklahoma to a music festival. My concern is that we were there on the wrong day!" The congregation laughed. They sounded like an extended family really enjoying one another's company.

Some years ago, I was invited to speak at the morning service of a small church in Indiana. Minutes before the service was to begin, the pastor and I met in a hallway behind the sanctuary. The organist began to play — the signal for us to enter by way of two doors and take our places on either side of the pulpit.

The pastor went through one door, and I opened another to find a rickety old stairway which I believed led me into the sanctuary. Instead I found myself upstairs in a semi-darkened room full of stored records and furniture. I could hear the organ thundering below. They are expecting me. I began to panic and search for another door. There wasn't any. Moments seemed like hours. I stumbled back to the hallway after falling flat from tripping over a chair, I'm certain the congregation thought that a giant rat had invaded their ceiling.

Hurriedly I found another door at the far end of the hallway, rushed up some steps and ran to my appointed seat. The music had stopped, I looked like a mess. My summer suit was crumpled and dirty.

But there's a good side to all of this. Somehow I felt that my disheveled appearance increased my appeal for mission funds. I kept my laughter to myself. I was truly enduring an unexpected Laurel and Hardy slapstick comedy, and I was the "fall guy."

Children add extra enjoyment to church. Isn't that how we seniors often remember some of the joy we experienced on a Sunday morning?

I laughingly recall the Sunday morning when our minister was preaching up a storm. In the congregation sat a young mother with her three year old, Caroline. The little girl squirmed out of her mother's arms and began plodding up and down the aisles, finally stopping below the minister who was looking Heavenward and shouting, "And God said, Yes, and God said." Then looking down he saw the little girl staring up at him. Concentrating on the

"I just love our new seniors' chapel!"

child, his trend of thought gone, he yelled . . . "and God said . . . madam if you don't come get your child I'm going to lose my mind!" The embarrassed mother ran to the front of the church and swept Caroline into her arms. The congregation laughed. I've forgotten the topic of his sermon, but I sure do remember that precious little child who brought joy to the whole congregation.

A Seniors Sunday School class met in a hall where a Saturday night fellowship dinner had been held the night before. Some balloons were still scattered around the room. As the teacher thumbed through his Bible, one retiree pinged a balloon across the table. Couples on both sides joined in keeping the balloon going back and forth. This lasted for about ten minutes when the teacher laughingly said, "Whatever the score, playtime is over, and let's get on with the lesson."

The joy of this fun-time brought back fond memories. All were reliving a part of their cherished childhood games. I expect to see some more of this balloon activity in that Sunday School. It sure unifies the troops.

What else can one do sometimes in church but laugh at one's self. It's long been known that God has a sense of humor. Look at you and me.

During my years of mission service in Africa, two of my students designed stained glass windows for a chapel. All was going well until one villager after looking at the design of God creating the world, exclaimed that the figure representing God looked like him. And it did. So much so that the design was rejected because it upset too many folks who knew the guy. Even humor invades our most well-intentioned plans, doesn't it?

Many pastors use humor to help their flocks understand their messages. There is such a person in Arkansas who is very much in demand as a speaker.

I asked him what his favorite story was and it goes this way:

He announces that he will preach on the sin of telling falsehoods, and then asks the question, "How many of you have read the 4th chapter of Habakkuk?"

Immediately several hands go up. And with a grin on his face he says, "It's you people I'm preaching to. You're lying. There's no fourth chapter in Habakkuk."

He's gotten their attention as he smiles to make another point, and you can bet your bottom dollar all are listening."

So with that I'll leave you to enjoy or moan over the following cartoons.

"Our pastor's afraid of water, and he's not taking any chances!"

*"The fact is, Reverend, that the older I get the less strength
I have to break the Ten Commandments!"*

"They didn't like my sermon!"

"I can bless your canary, Myrtle, but I can't baptize it!"

"Wilbur's lost his voice!"

WORLD'S HIGHEST PULPIT

ELEVATOR

"He seems a little out of touch!"

52

"Delbert, I know you want to evangelize ranches in Texas, but . . ."

Keeping Cool on the Social Circuit

I have on my kitchen cabinet a calendar of witty sayings that spark good common sense. One that caught my attention is "Grow old by wearing out, not rusting out." Wearing out suggests to me using our energies for positive reasons. It's a refreshing kind of tiredness as we enjoy being with our friends..

One cardinal rule for maintaining friends is never to let them know that you've heard them tell their jokes for the umpteenth time. They'll ask you if you've ever heard this one or that one. And it's kind to reply that you'd enjoy hearing it. The fun is watching them laugh themselves to tears. How many times have you told the same joke to the same friends? You'll never know probably, because they won't tell you.

One prime social event many enjoy is dancing. It's fun to make up steps as clumsy as they may be, and then within earshot of other dancers on the floor tell your partner how great it is that you learned your new steps in Venezuela or some other exotic place. This will make your performance on the dance floor if not acceptable, hopefully tolerated. The really good professional dancers appreciate people like me because I make them look even better. They can show their students what not to do. But for me the whole idea is to have fun.

I've come up with a new way to evaluate dance music. It's how many calories a person burns dancing to a particular tune for so many minutes. For example, a Viennese waltz would be announced from the bandstand as a 250 calorie melody while an extremely slow fox trot would be fifty. This would tip the dancers off as to whether they have the energy to do it, go to the bathroom or try to chat above the blaring sounds of the orchestra.

Most of us enjoy good conversation when we dine out. Sometimes this becomes impossible even with our hearing aids turned up because of the loud disco music, nerve wracking clatter of dishes and continuous raucous laughter.

Have you ever been in a restaurant where you try to guess what your friends are saying, and you can't hear them because of the noise? Also your meal has been served, and you can't just get up and walk out. It's really a tough situation.

What might solve the problem, is to have lip reading classes at senior centers. Wouldn't this hold the younger generations spellbound as they watch us having an intelligent conversation while having a meal, and they can't hear a thing. Most can't anyway because of the years of the overbearing boom and beat of rock taking its toll on their generation's hearing.

"Sometimes, dear, it pays to suffer memory loss like forgetting to wear our hearing aids!"

Another conversational aid would be use a set of cue cards that we can show one another with words like yes, no, ha-ha, that's good, or hold-up-your-card-where-I-can-see-it. We'd have to keep our conversations short, sweet and simple with as few words as possible, but that's not all bad. We would have more time to eat and chew. Aren't doctors encouraging us to chew twenty-some times per bite to improve our digestion.My guess is that the answer is to seek out a quiet restaurant and to heck with being seen at a noisy expensive place.

The art of keeping "cool" can be trying if your wife or date sees another wearing the same dress right down to the last pleat and spangle. You men have to be very creative to handle this situation to avoid embarrassment. One way is to start a rumor that a new stunning dress is being worn by several attractive models to demonstrate how it compliments women of different sizes and shapes. Another tactic is to keep the ladies separated from one another as far as possible. This can be difficult if you both have reserved tables next to one another. It's more manageable if you can maneuver your lady into a "safe zone" in a crowd or on the dance floor. The problem is you're on the run all evening, and that's not much fun.

On the other hand, just forget the whole thing. Enjoy the evening. Chances are you don't know the other person wearing the same dress, and will probably never see them again. In any event, two women can be proud that they agree on a dress that fits their personalities and makes them look great!

America's number one social event is eating with friends. Retired folks really turn out to a pot-luck supper. It beats restaurant food anytime and is most often more wholesome and a lot cheaper. It attracts larger crowds to church and club meetings. Who was it that said, "Feed my sheep?"

Isn't it fun to take our very own dish to one of these meals and enjoy the compliments for our generations' old family recipe! How they all laugh when we reveal our secret that it's really a Sara Lee store-bought dessert warmed up and transplanted into our Corning Ware.

After a fellowship dinner we harmonize with our friends singing some old favorite songs that take us back to our "good old days." Are you like me? When I'm singing, I hope everyone's singing so they can hide all my mistakes.

Isn't that what life is all about, sharing our mistakes in fun and laughter?

"Dennis, I'm getting worried about or relationship!"

"Does your Medicare cover jitterbugging?"

"My wife was a captain in World War II!"

"Please play louder. She's telling me about her operation for the fourth time!"

"It all started forty years ago when she yelled 'jump'!"

Laughing Around the House
— Be Your Own Comedian —

The basement in our rural home in Arksansas began to flood. It was a real frog-strangling rain. Water poured in from around a pipe connecting our house to the well. It was awful. Something had to be done. Water was spreading all over.

My wife, Evelyn, immediately took charge in controlling the inflow of water by rigging up a funnel made of aluminum foil attached to a hose which drained into a floor outlet in a storage room. It worked perfectly. So what it if looked like a Rube Goldberg contraption. The problem was solved. Even a builder and plumber who later surveyed the situation marveled at Evelyn's ingenuity.

Then came the fun. My office was in our home. I had a part-time secretary, a lady in her seventies who did excellent typing and record keeping. Together we prepared a degree in Engineering, a large official-looking diploma on parchment and invited Evelyn to her "graduation."

Evelyn was not her normal self during the presentation. She was totally speechless at first, and then began to laugh. We joined in. It turned a day of disaster into a time of joy.

When I married Evelyn I inherited her adopted daughter, a brilliant young lady who is now a veterinarian. We noticed that she loved pets and had a special talent in caring for them. After she completed her first year of high school in our town, we enrolled her in a rural high school about a thirty minute drive from our home. It had an excellent farm livestock program, much better than the school she had attended. She loved it, and promptly began raising pigs to show at county and state fairs.

Unbeknown to me, one day she brought home a piglet, the runt of the litter. The small critter was having problems getting enough milk. Returning home from my university classes one mid-afternoon, I entered the living room. Evelyn was rocking what I thought to be a baby wrapped in a blanket and sucking a bottle. Surprised, I tiptoed over and pulled back the blanket to see the piglet sucking and smacking. With a sly grin, I turned to Evelyn and said, "Honey, it doesn't look like me!" We laughed until we cried.

Evelyn died a few years ago from a massive heart attack while we were in Florida. I still remember our days of swine and roses. What joy a piglet brought into our lives. It bonded us together even more.

The lesson I continually learn is that life is full of opportunities to share those many funny incidents in our lives with family, friends and strangers.

How many of you have ever had dinner together at home where you have improvised the setting to resemble an expensive night club? You prepare a menu which lists such delicacies as Charred Zambesi Zebra with Shakespearean Pudding, and you're only serving hamburgers with vanilla ice cream. As for evening attire, you can be dressed very informally in jeans with the man sporting a bow tie and Tee-shirt and the lady adorned with several outlandish necklaces complemented by earrings completely out of place. A lighted candle on top of an inverted saucer and some softly playing taped music complete the scene of fantasy.

As for conversation, you can pretend to be ambassadors in a foreign country or wherever your imaginations soar into creative fun. We've done this in my home. I still remember dining at the "Top of the Mark" in San Francisco, and I've never actually been there.

Did you ever give your spouse or friend a "his and her" candy bar? Try it. You merely put the word "his" on one half and "her" on the other, and pass it back and forth, as you eat it together.

Want to add some zest to the old home front? Carry copies of jokes home with you. Search your newspapers and magazines for humor. Then adapt this fun and nonsense to your style of telling the story. There's no doubt about it, good humor can strengthen a relationship every day.

Do you recall the days of door-to-door salespeople? One salesman knocked at the front door of a man I know very well. My friend was wearing an apron and holding a large spoon as he opened the door. He was preparing lunch for his wife. "Is the lady of the house in?", the salesman asked. "Speaking!", the husband replied.

That's the kind of humor I'm talking about. So go to it, friends.

"If anyone calls, tell them I'm in surgery."

"I'll mow, dear, when I finish my tea."

"Jake, stop that nonsense. I know you hate doing laundry."

"Somehow, I feel we're not welcome!"

"Not speaking today, eh?"

"John, I'm going to call the National Enquirer. When you tense your knee, it looks like Bill Clinton!"

"I asked him if it was too late for the garbage pickup, and all he said was 'Hop in'!"

Continuing Education — Keeping Our Minds from Going To Sleep

There seems to be quite a debate about us older folks. One is that we're too old to learn. "You can't teach an old dog new tricks,:" they say.

Others claim that we're never too old to learn unless we're ravaged by diseases that destroy our ability to remember. However, science has shown that we older people can be pretty sharp mentally and can continue to learn.

I like to keep up on the world, don't you? Questions like "Who invented plum pudding?" or "How big can a dinosaur egg be?" or "Which American president snored the loudest?" Who knows when such information will come in handy to let others know that we can contribute to the conversation and can change the subject when arguments get out of control.

As we grow older, the sport of sitting and people-watching becomes predominant. Along with that comes conversation. That's where we have to get prepared to get our two cents in every conversation. We don't want to appear dumb. We suddenly change the subject to get in our licks while our memory tape expands into impressive vagueness. No one really wants to challenge us because we are using combinations of multi-syllable words that get everyone totally confused and lost just as we are. It's when we talk in simple English that it becomes dangerous. People begin to know what we think.

It's amazing the number of people who will turn out for a lecture on a subject they've never really thought about. I remember one such lecture. It was "The Control of the Blood Flow of the Vervet Monkey." That's a subject that will cause people to be amazed at anyone knowing anything about it. They will recognize "monkey," and that's about it.

I have learned that some subjects are real tough to work into a conversation. For example, the art of preparing Congolese salted caterpillars, or how I built my clubhouse when I was twelve. However, I've discovered that a prolonged lull in conversation signals that the trend of thought has expired, and it's an opportunity to jump in with anything.

What better way is there to keep our mental trivia store brimming full than by attending an elderhostel or joining a tour for anywhere. If you love

"Well I'll be . . . Spain . . . 1961!
I never forget a nose!"

73

to travel you can relive the days of Stanley and Livingstone in Africa or dance with the Navajo in Arizona.

Years ago I helped lead a group to East Africa. One of our group, a charming little lady, a university librarian, bought a pith helmet and safari suit in Nairobi. What a triumphal reentry she made on her return to the States and reported on her adventures of visiting the slave cave, the impoverished market place and Livingstone's home in Zanzibar!

Sometimes our quest for knowledge can be very trying. Such was my situation in Zanzibar where I was taking two elderly ladies on a walking tour around the island. In the maze of narrow streets I got totally lost, I had no idea where we were or how far we were from our hotel. Both women said that their feet were killing them. If we didn't end this walking tour soon, I'd have to carry them. Then lo and behold, we stumbled upon a beach area quite by accident and found our bus. I can still hear them extolling my virtues as a knowledgeable guide. They will never know how dumb I felt.

At a recent elderhostel, I learned that it's best to avoid mid-afternoon lectures if one wants to keep the troops focused on the subject discussed. Believe it or not, in an afternoon session on big band music with a tape blaring "American Patrol," a few of the men dropped off to sleep. When you gotta' nap, you gotta' nap!

Speaking about keeping awake brought me back to Las Cruces, New Mexico, where I was speaking on life in rural Africa. From my raised lectern I got a good look at my audience.

Over to my right, sitting near the front, was a married couple. The wife appeared to be hanging on to every word I said. But her husband was sound asleep with his arms down to his side, and he was snoring.

I saw her glance at him, thoroughly disgusted. Then in perfect composure, she swung her left elbow hard right into his solar plexus. He became totally awake with a glassy stare towards the ceiling. I know he was in terrible pain. First from his wife, but even more from my speech which he could now hear.

Perhaps my most trying moment in learning how people outside the United States live and think occurred in Macao. Some Portuguese friends invited me to attend a Mardi Gras Ball as their guest.

"I believe I'll have a nap while you kids tour the castle!"

It was a formal affair. I had no tuxedo to wear. It was too late to find one. My friends then presented me with a "domino," a clown suit with mask, saying that this was an acceptable option for dress. I wore it.

But, would you believe it! I was the only man in costume other than the gypsy orchestra leader. By midnight, the glazed glances of the totally saturated diplomatic corps assured me that I was properly attired. They were all seeing one another as a bunch of clowns. The one thing I did not wear was the black mask. I was afraid that it would look like a hold-up, and that's no way to make friends.

Have you noticed how our curiosity leads us into exploring fascinating subjects? We become motivated by our need to be unique and leave our mark on posterity. Once I stayed in the home of a man who had a theory why much of America is stressed out. He said: "It's tomatoes! They're poisoning our system. Too much acid. Give 'em up before they kill you!"

As he expounded shaking his fist at me, I noticed that his wife and daughter left the room. I didn't dare tell him how many tomatoes I had eaten that day. It might have caused a heart attack, and his attending physician would report "He died thinking about tomatoes."

Yes, I keep learning the darndest things in the most unexpected places. And if you're having problems with your kids and grandchildren, have you ever thought it might be tomatoes?

"Oh, oh! I believe we have a clown in our group!"

CHINESE WARRIOR

After Taxes

Hall Duncan

79

"Now that I've answered the 'big question' . . .
I'll get on with the lecture!"

EASTER ISLAND

"Oh my! I just remembered. I forgot my nap today!"

My Body Left My Mind
For A Seven Day Cruise!

The Cruise! Water, sun, mountains of food, impeccable service! I was under the spell of total relaxation. My mind stayed behind in Miami.

Seven days of floating. Not just the traveling part but the idyllic feel of the ship. I never walked anywhere, I floated as if on a cushion of air. As I moved repeatedly from open deck and sun to food, lots of food.

There is never a meal time really, although we all go to the dining room at appointed times. We continually graze from one exotic "pasture" on one deck to the next. And if you, like me, aren't hungry but we paid for it, then we're going to get our money's worth even if it makes us ill.

By the third day at sea, numbness sets in. A benign out-of-this world feeling affirms that there is a "Heaven on earth," and this floating paradise must be a foretaste of what the good afterlife is like. No wonder a Pharaoh buried his royal "barge" near his pyramid to keep his cruising dream alive when he would sail one day down the "Nile in the sky." I'm sure he kept a lot of exquisite cuisine aboard.

The nights were full of glitter and excitement as the Tommy Dorsey Band struck up, I wished I had learned to dance within a four foot square or smaller. A compressed version of West Coast Swing would have come in very handy. The dance floor was small. The management preferred that you would enjoy the music more if you sat, drank a lot and listened.

I call dancing on a cruise, "postage stamp" dancing, as many press to claim a tiny shuffling domain on the crowded floor. If you really want togetherness, dance. Chances are you will have changed partners several times during the crush. "Where are you, Lois?" "Over here doing the waltz!" "Good heavens, whom am I with?" "I'll meet you at the bandstand after this number."

It's interesting to see how a mass of packed bodies begins to resemble a huge centipede trying to move in a circular direction. Lois and I like to be on the edge where we have a chance to breathe, check our legs and feet for any bruises, and escape from all this closeness. But it's fun!

The Captain's dinner is something to behold. Lois and I are suddenly propelled into high society. Washington, eat your heart out! The maneuvering to sit with the captain is fun to watch. One tip is that if you really want to sit at "the table," shortly after boarding circulate a lots of rumors about your "astounding accomplishments" whether real or

"And now our latest s-s-s-mash hit, the 'Sardine Hop'!"

imaginary. Invent thrilling stories about finding a mastodon alive in the Arctic Circle, or that you're interviewing great sea captains for your new unpublished book already backed by Hollywood. Even if you are discovered as a fake and thrown into the brig, you still have a great story. The public will eat it up.

No, we weren't at the Captain's table. We behaved ourselves. We did notice one elderly gentleman wearing his full dress military officer uniform. He was immediately ushered to "the table." I wouldn't dare wear my Private First Class infantry outfit. I can't possibly button the jacket or pants!

Evening dress is always interesting. Some folks plan months ahead what fashion statement they will make at the Captain's dinner. I enjoy it all because each person is revealing part of their unique personality. One lady wore a black dress which looked as though it had survived a shark attack from the belt up. I wish more had latched on to that style. It would have provided us a lot more entertainment.

Physical fitness isn't completely ignored on a cruise. A few passengers are up at dawn to circle the jogging path followed by a workout in the gym. But the majority feel they will worry about their weight later back home.

I especially admire the stewards who keep a semblance of sanity and maintain safety for us passengers. Our table steward told me that he was looking forward to getting home to the Dominican Republic for a few weeks vacation and his "real" world. He didn't need to see the extravagant floor shows and other entertainment aboard ship. We were his entertainment as we plodded to his table lost in a world of total serenity.

I'm rather anxious to meet up with my mind which I left in Miami. I wonder if it will accept my body, now ten pounds heavier. I've got to get back into a world where I have to think. Gosh, that's a tiresome thought! How soon can I take another cruise?

*"Agnes always makes a big scene
when the band asks for requests!"*

"My husband sees art in everything he does on this cruise!"

"I don't know why, but this end of the ship reminds me of Noah's Ark!"

"There goes next year's cruise!"

Hall Duncan

"I just loved it when my doctor said to have lots of water with light meals!"

It's Not A Bad Idea When
Your Life's Going To The Dogs

Let's face it. Pets are child substitutes. As we grow older they often become mate substitutes either when we're single or just bored to death with our one-and-only.

I've had some first hand experience on communication confusion with a dog in my house. My late wife, Evelyn, and I had a docile, sweet dispositioned housebroken female Sheltie. Her name was Babe. She slept on our bed, sometimes between us on the top covers, and at other times sprawled over my feet, locking me into one sleeping position for the night. If I were dog tired it didn't make any difference. I became dead to the world.

But, if I were restless, I was in for a tough night. If I left Babe anchored on my feet, my legs would sweat profusely under that dog heat, especially on a summer night. The pretzel position I assumed made me stiff when I woke in the morning.

However, my major problem was that our dog's name was "Babe." It was my name also when Evelyn wanted to address me in her most endearing manner.

Everytime Evelyn yelled "Babe" the dog and I would jump. We wouldn't know what Evelyn wanted until we could see her hands. If she held the dog food bowl or a squeaky toy, we knew who was on call. Or did we? Was I to feed the dog, play with it or leave it alone? We were often confused.

One solution that eased my situation was to stay a good distance from Babe during her evening feeding which was regular as clockwork. Evelyn was so organized.

When Babe was out in the yard playing and we were indoors, and Evelyn softly said, "Babe!", I knew I was the chosen one at the moment. Ah, memories!

My experience with pets has been quite bizarre at times. I remember having supper with a couple and their seven year old daughter in South Africa. The father, a minister of the Presbyterian church, after a short blessing, was startled to see a duckling suddenly waddle around the table

"About your new suit for the dance tonight . . .
I have something to tell you!"

top in between the vegetables and bread plates. His daughter had sneaked her pet duck on to the dining table, to join us for the meal.

I remember the father saying: "Gillian, if that duck does what I think it's going to do, you are in big, big trouble." Upon that, Gillian snatched up the duckling and put it out in the yard. It's the first time I ever had a live duck for supper.

People's lives do change when pets completely take over. A friend of mine in West Virginia married a man who loved his hunting dogs. So much so that he wouldn't sell or give away any of them. The very thought of losing one nagged him. Their home was inundated by dogs under the chairs, behind the lamps, and all over the kitchen. I counted over fifteen. All were reported to be house-broken. But they were never quite sure about that.

Dog food was stored in sacks under the bed in the master bedroom. The house smelled like a dogfood factory. In fact everyone smelled like dog food. No wonder the dogs hung around inside the house all the time.

The thing that caused me to be concerned about my friend's husband was when he would take his dogs out for a lurch. Yes, I said lurch. Because it was impossible to walk with them, with as many as seven attached to his belt. He was jerked into pulsating lurches, in random directions. I became terribly tempted to whistle and excite the dogs to a flat-out run and see what would happen. But I didn't dare. I'll bet if I had my friend would be eternally grateful because her husband would have sold off all but one before he came home from the hospital.

Being a cartoonist affords some rare insights into human behavior and pets. Early one evening I was called to the home of tax lobbyist who hired me to do a political cartoon for him. As we planned the sketch, I heard the weirdest wail coming from his front bedroom.

I asked "What was that?" "It's our pet parrot singing," he said, "Come and look." So we went to the bedroom door where I saw his wife sitting up in bed as pregnant as everything, playing a ukulele and singing with their pet parrot. His explanation was that this was the one thing that kept her calm until it was time to take her to the hospital to have her baby.

This last experience proved to me that the old expression, "That's for the birds," has a lot of truth in it! It's amazing what pets do for people. Remember your pet frog or butterfly when you were a kid?

"Keeping up with your dog!"

*"Agnes, I hate your
lets-all-have-a-nice-treat arrangement!"*

"It's not funny, William!"

"Now that's what I call 'togetherness'!"

"Let's see now . . . Who goes with whom!"

"DOG SHOW"

Hall Duncan

Retreading Around
The Retirement Village

It's enjoyable to observe the comings and goings around the retirement village. News abounds unexpectedly in such a tightly knit community. Everyone is a reporter and newspaper at the same time. Whatever happens from brushing teeth to gargling at four in the morning becomes common knowledge immediately.

Card games sometimes become activities of extreme contention, and one is advised to wear soccer shin guards when playing the residents hell-bent for winning. Scrabble provides hilarious entertainment as some sly characters invent new words such as zebear, and glibly try to explain it's the offspring of a zebra and a bear. But most older folks are real sharp in protecting their turf. They know who their real friends are.

At one assisted living center I met a gentleman resident whose interest in fun won him the honor of being the "unofficial mayor." He loved humor and laughter and went out on his own to organize an evening of fun and laughter. Some laughed who for months had never cracked a smile. He helped them to wake up the little kid within themselves and enjoy the healing power of positive fun.

Did you hear about the elderly lady at a rest home who was heard to be talking to someone in her room late one night? The administrator informed her that she shouldn't have visitors after ten at night. She emphatically said she didn't and explained she had adopted a cockroach as a pet and talked to it. This called for an immediate investigation. Her room was sprayed with insecticide. They never found the cockroach. As she watched the whole procedure, a sly grin came over her face. She had won again against the system.

One of the big adjustments in living in a retirement village is that as you move from the bungalow/duplex to the apartment to the small single room and then to intensive care, your living space gets smaller and smaller. So maybe spayed and neutered pet mice or even cockroaches aren't such a bad idea after all for constant companionship.

One great advantage to living in such a place is that if you do some cooking for yourself, try preparing some fun exotic dish . You can serve it to your friends and neighbors. Then watch them before you take a bite.

"Betty Jean, since you want me to bite your neck,
I'm going to my room to get my teeth."

You'll know if you have a winner or not. It's kind of like the African chief who has members of his court test his food against poisoning.

And speaking about food I heard about one resident who complained that her potato was bad. She wailed that it was awful. One nurse was called to her side to take the heat of her anger. The nurse, being a quick-minded humorist, swept the potato off the plate and spanked it soundly saying "Bad potato, bad potato." The complaining resident was dumbfounded. The crisis was over.

As you and I grow older we meet people who are seeking to be retreaded to add more years of enjoyable living to their lives and to others around them. It all gets back to attitude. To seek and practice positive thoughts and activities which keep us fun to be around.

We all have to take the medicines and follow the recommendations of the doctors we trust and in whose hands we place our lives. Why not take a further step if you haven't done so already.

Add a daily dosage of humor to your life. I guarantee it will generate a deep healing feeling within yourself. As you share your smiling attitude and witty stories with your neighbors and room-mates, you'll soon have the reputation of being the humor doctor around your retirement place.

When your phone rings for your advice on how to have a more healthy life, you can answer like my good friend, Lyn Hester, does:

"Take two laughs and call me in the morning!"

"Reader's Digest says it's a sign of super intelligence."

"Eleanor, I can't seem to find my socks!"

"Gloria will now hum 'Love Is A Many Splendored Thing' in Italian, Russian and English <u>simultaneously!</u>"

"I know you don't like this, dear. Think of it as commercial poetry!"

"Could you show your love for me, Calvin, in some other way than home repairs?"

"It's as if we don't have enough stress around here."

The Dating Game . . .
Only A Little Slower

One romance that warms my heart happened in Tulsa, Oklahoma. It's all about Paul, a friend of mine, whose wife died after forty-eight years of marriage.

One of his favorite activities was singing with the Over the Hill Gang, a group of senior citizens who enjoyed harmonizing together. It was in this group he met Oma, a very attractive lady who had lost her husband to leukemia.

It wasn't long until Paul fell in love with Oma. His longing for her to be his wife increased daily as they would walk together with other seniors in a large shopping mall.

How was he to propose? The romance was blossoming. He noticed that each morning they would walk by a bakery that sold large cookies. "That's it," he thought, "I'll write my marriage proposal on a big cookie prominently displayed in the window." And he did. His message read: "Oma, will you marry me?" Paul made certain that Oma saw the cookie.

Four months later to the day, Oma replied on her big cookie, "Paul, Yes, Yes with joy! When?" They were soon married and are enjoying lots of fun and laughter in their retirement years. Even a recent trip down the Amazon! It all began to happen because of Paul's sense of humor and great creativity expressing his love for Oma.

Recently I had the pleasure of leading a discussion group of university students on what they look for when selecting a mate. All expressed their need for a spouse with a healthy sense of humor, that strengthens their marriage.

It's fun to listen to seniors who are searching for companionship of the opposite sex. The women compare men "who give them the eye." The men do likewise. It always comes down to a question of compatibility beyond the eye contact to the final meeting. Laughing at oneself can open doors to lasting friendships and even marriage.

One situation involving two senior singles I'm aware of is a retired school teacher who told a retired professor how perfect he was. He was absolutely flattered and with a smile accepted the compliment saying,

"I got your call, Jenny. What's on your mind?"

absolutely flattered and with a smile accepted the compliment saying, "Jesus, move over,!" Both laughed 'til they cried.

Creativity in matchmaking is the name of the game. Try composing a silly opera while doing dishes together, or put on a tour guide cap when taking your lady out for a drive. Keep a few clean cartoons and family jokes in your pocket for out-to-dinner conversation and look for the fun side of everything you do together.

Dancing is something to behold as a senior dating couple fantasize on the dance floor as they glide or chug to the beat of the melody. It's all a matter of having fun and not trying to compete with the professional dance instructors floating around the perimeter of the floor. They may wonder who's teaching you those crazy steps. Keep 'em guessing.

And should you find the sounds abrasive in a restaurant, take some cotton along for you and your date, stuff it in your ears, and then have fun trying to read one another's lips. Be sure your eyeglasses are clean. I tried this lip-reading thing with friends in a disco in Mexico City. I didn't strain my voice and none of us really knew what the other was talking about.

Most of us as we reach the 60's and 70's in age find that a nap before going out for the evening is a must. At dinner you can sure tell those who didn't have one because they drop off immediately after or during dessert, well before the music program and guest speaker get underway.

The motto today for a happy post fifty-five marriage, is "Those who nap together stay together!" Adequate rest is all important to having the energy to grab all the gusto you can.

One last bit of advice from our retirees group. If you're single and want to enjoy being with your date, remember the time it took for you to do things when you were in high school and multiply that time by four. You'll be able to whoop it up at a pace you can live and laugh with.

"What a night, Curtis! You're so romantic! You've even trimmed your nostrils!"

"Regarding your marriage proposal to me, Herman, I have four things to discuss with you this afternoon."

"Honey, we have so much in common. We've both
been recycled by the same doctor!"

"We'll take it. It's a perfect fit for watching football games!"

"And, Lord, I do love Widow Jones, but please tell her 'no more broccoli pie'!"

"Gertrude's directing our church singles' Nativity Play, and I don't believe she likes me."

There's Still A Twinkle In The Twilight!

When all seems lost and life's light appears to be dimming, it's time to cope with hope and ease the pain and stress with some humor.

I have a friend, Ralph, who is retired. He became blind from an incurable disease a few years ago. But his "golden" years continue to be "golden". He teaches Sunday School once or twice a month. He is blessed with a loving wife, Jayne. He loves to travel, keenly sensing the smells, sounds and touches along the way.

Humor is an important part of his happiness. He gains much of his strength listening to humorous tapes. He enjoys telling folks about his one big benefit: Jayne can park them in a handicap space at Wal-Mart. Ralph doesn't want pity. He feeds on laughter. It's medicine for him. He loves it.

There are several other people who have inspired me on the importance of the gift of laughter. Take Lucille, for instance, in her eighties, plagued by throat cancer and terminally ill.

She saw an article in the local paper about my work with senior citizens and called me to come and visit with her about the bygone days when I drew cartoons for her husband's advertising agency. We soon developed a renewed friendship of laughing about our memories.

On one occasion I found out that Lucille loved soft chocolates without nuts. So my friend, Lois, and I visited her as comical doctors. We brought her our prescription. A box of soft chocolates, to take as needed. As I handed her the chocolates, I said "Lucille, you've got to have nuts with these!" Then Lois and I uncovered some signs we were each wearing marked NUTS. Lucille just laughed and laughed. We knew that for that moment there was joy that overcame the pain she was enduring.

Several months later Lucille died. At her graveside funeral service I shall never forget the happiness we all felt about Lucille's effect upon our lives as we released balloons with our personal messages honoring her. They gently soared into the southern sky. Lucille was going home laughing.

My mother died from intestinal cancer when I was sixteen. It was a devastating blow to my father and me and my two younger brothers. Years later I "adopted" an elderly lady, Edith Beal, to be my mother. We had a

"Your late husband was a bit of a show-off, wasn't he?"

marvelous relationship as "mother and son" during the years before I moved out of the state. She loved the gifts I brought her from different countries where I lectured.

I last saw Edith when she hadn't long to live. Being a student of ventriloquism, I took my green frog puppet to cheer her up. I told her that she had another visitor, and introduced her to my frog. Her eyes sparkled as she glanced back and forth from the frog to my lips. She smiled as I had never seen her smile in a long time. Pain was put aside for a little while.

One of my favorite stories about humor when life is really tough was sent to me by a hospital chaplain in Oregon. A lady was confined to her hospital bed and had to be fed by tubes through her nose. A very painful annoying procedure.

She was concerned about receiving sufficient nourishment. She asked her doctor and nurse, "Am I getting enough good food?" "The best!" they said. She replied she was glad to hear that, and then invited them to be her guests for supper that night in her hospital room. Then with a naughty chuckle, she added, "When you come, you'd better bring your tubes!" Now that's the healing power of laughter taking place!

Here's how humor is helping Dan, a retired naval officer. I'm indebted him and his wife, Charleen, for their permission to quote the following from their Christmas newsletter. "*In March Dan had his right leg amputated below the knee. After hearing horror stories of wrong leg amputation, he took no chances and wrote 'NO' on the good leg and 'YES, CUT HERE,' on his bad leg. The doctor followed instructions!*

But, he got an infection in the hospital, and in April had to have it cleaned out, and more bone removed, and the wound left open to heal. It is healing nicely, but slowly. Now he is busy finding hospital, doctor, nurse and one-legged jokes! He says he can go to Halloween contests as Captain Silver with a real peg-leg — or stand on a street corner with a tin cup! Sometimes his mind is sicker than his body!!"

Both Dan and Charleen have a tremendous sense of humor in getting through some tough times. It's a great part of their healing!

This last true story sums it all up. Laughter can heal in a way nothing else can when it's done in loving fun! As one sage put it with a twinkle in his eye, "When you get to the end of your rope, tie a knot and hang on!"

124

"And furthermore, your late wife wills you this tape recording of her laughter to play always after your hilarious stories about Aunt Mary."

"I know it seems unusual, but this is what she always wanted"

"It gives me a totally new perspective on 'winging it'!"

"When God calls one of us up yonder, I believe I'll be a greeter at Wal-Mart!"

"We're out of food, Jill. But . . . ha . . . ha . . . we still have some very big leftovers!"

"When I get well what will you and our grandkids do for entertainment?"

Heavenly Days and Eternal Laughter

Heaven must be a fun place! You don't have to worry about what to wear when you go to a Jokers Club there. Just wear your undying smile.

I'm really overwhelmed when I think about the eternal reservoir of jokes in Heaven dating back to the first grunts of our cavemen ancestors learning to laugh. Can't you just imagine St. Paul sharing a yarn with David Livingstone and Queen Cleopatra! And there are no cultural or language barriers. The punch line comes through in a flash as they think funny stories to one another.

Sometimes I feel the presence of a family loved one who now resides in Heaven and I burst out laughing. I recall one such moment with my father when I tried to clean out hundreds of ants that had invaded our electric toaster. I used a box of ant powder to get rid of them. It was a mess. Then dad peered over with a sheepish grin that confirmed my stupidity and asked, "Why didn't you plug it in?". We laughed as I cleaned up the mess. I rarely look at a toaster without laughing and thinking of my father.

I like the gentle ways of some older folks who exclaim "for Heaven's sake," when something stressful happens. They are more prone to perceive some holy humor in the situation.

As we say farewell for now at a friend's funeral, have you noticed how we all gather around recalling the fun and hilarious moments we shared with the deceased? I'm sure they too are laughed with us.

We best remember those with whom we have laughed. It's another way, I believe, in telling one another how much we love them as friends. I realize more each day that God has a great sense of humor because He created laughter in you and me.

Saint Peter beamed a message down to me as I prepared this book. He reminded me that God is growing weary of lawyer and aggie jokes. However, he added, He loves the ones we and our loved ones have lived because they get better and better each year.

"You're both welcome, but please no lawyer jokes."

How often do we feel forsaken by God, when our prayers go unanswered or not in a way we wanted?

My minister told about such a case involving Abe, a devout Jewish gentleman who prayed incessantly for God to help him win the New York lottery. For years he prayed. For years he never won. Then one day Abe got so fed up, he cried out, "God, why haven't you answered my prayer? Why? Why?" And then God said, "You haven't cooperated with me, Abe. You have to buy a ticket."

So keep living and exercising your laughter. You'll be in great shape for Heaven.

"Myrtle, you made it!
We gave up on you when
you belched at the prayer breakfast!"

135

"Sweetie, your fuel tank is too heavy for your lift-off!"

"Dear Mary: Remember when we used to float the Buffalo River, well . . ."

137

"You've got to be careful calling one another 'Angel'
or you'll be hugged to death!"

"Your Honor, Granny was only flying five billion miles an hour in a four billion passing zone!"

"Have you had your shots?"

"Heaven is so much more peaceful and quiet since Clyde's halo slipped."

You Haven't Changed A Bit!
Maybe A Little!

How many time have you heard this? I love it, particularly if I've gained unnecessary pounds, and I know they're lying through their teeth. But it's kind lying. That's what we older folks revel in. I believe if kind fibbing doesn't add years to our lives, it certainly adds quality and lots of laughs. I'm convinced God doesn't see this as wrong. We've just become full of Irish blarney.

Last spring I watched a couple in their late eighties (full of affection for one another) gently circle the dance floor. The tune was a slow waltz. Suddenly the band exploded with Glen Miller's "In The Mood." This rejuvenated twosome immediately began jumping and twirling to the accelerated syncopated beat like the two highschool seniors they were when they first met. Their bodies couldn't keep up with their brain signals of earlier years. But they tried, and without any embarrassment had fun.

One didn't have to guess what they were thinking. It was all in their eyes and carefree laughter. They were "going-on-ninety" years young.

In recognizing friends who go way back in my life, I recall their mannerisms of how they tweak their ear or rub their chin. But it's always the look — the sparkle in their eyes that's my main clue. How wonderful it is to see their eyes dance with laughter, a sure sign of friendship.

"You haven't changed a bit!", our friends say to us, and we love it!

True Love!

International Center For HUMOR AND HEALTH

The International Center for Humor and Health is dedicated to spreading the healing art of laughter and improving communities through the use of humor.

Humor and health education seminars, conferences, workshops and lectures are provided for all ages and needs. The Center's inner-city youth programs feature summer camps, after school activities and community service.

The Center's clowning ministry visits hospitals, nursing homes and retirement centers. Others assist in humor research, publish books and training materials, and participate in humor for health exhibits.

The Center's National Clown and Laughter Hall of Fame inducts deserving individuals who have contributed their talents of humor for a more healthy world physically, mentally and spiritually.

The International Center for Humor and Health, established in 1988 as the National Clown and Laughter Hall of Fame, is a unique not-for-profit, 501(c)(3) organization using non-traditional ways to relieve and resolve community problems.

Are You Interested?

- In having the Center help you and your organization, club or church.
- or sponsoring or donating to one of our programs.

CALL: 405-341-8115

OR WRITE: International Center for Humor and Health
2930 Hidden Valley Road
Edmond, OK 73013 USA

e-mail: humor@ionet.net

Fax: 405-341-8240